T0197378

Presented to:

_____

_____

Also by Gina M. Dahl: Three Sneaky Emotions, One Powerful You!

Choices, Choices Everywhere!

Written and Illustrated by
Gina M. Dahl

WestBow Press books may be ordered through booksellers or by contacting:

WestBow Press
A Division of Thomas Nelson & Zondervan
1663 Liberty Drive
Bloomington, IN 47403
www.westbowpress.com
844-714-3454

ISBN: 978-1-4497-7547-6 (sc)
ISBN: 978-1-4497-7548-3 (e)

Library of Congress Control Number: 2012921307

Print information available on the last page.

WestBow Press rev. date: 02/22/2023

WESTBOW
PRESS®
A DIVISION OF THOMAS NELSON
& ZONDERVAN

For children everywhere

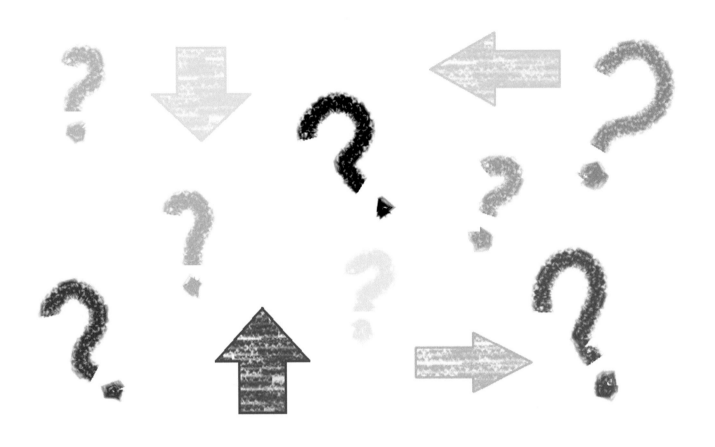

Choices, choices everywhere!

From what we eat...

...to what we wear,

We choose choices all the time.
You choose yours, and I choose mine.

It matters what we choose and why,
as we grow each day,
from where we go, to what we do,
to what we think and say.

Every choice starts with a thought,
and leads to actions in the link,
to habits, to character, to destiny.
So, be careful what you think!

Whether we want good or bad,
to come out from our lives,
is really up to us.
So, choosing carefully is wise!

Good choices lead to good,
and peace is sure to follow...

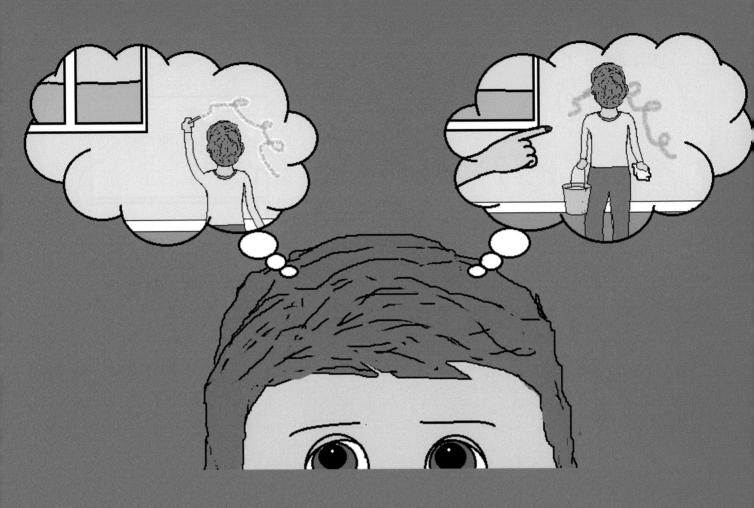

...but bad choices lead to bad,
and cause sadness, pain, and sorrow.

Sometimes bad things happen,
that are not of our own choice...

...but we can see things change,
when we praise God and rejoice.

The things we choose to see,
as most important to us now,
can either lead to blessing,
or trouble someday, somehow.

**If we're in a situation,
and not sure what choice is best,
God gives us wisdom when we ask,
and helps us with the rest.**

**God knows we make mistakes.
He chose to forgive us long ago.
And if we believe what He says,
His Love in our hearts we can know.**

If you choose to think on God's Words,
believing what He says is true,
and include Him in your choices,
then, you'll see His best for you!

Printed in the United States
by Baker & Taylor Publisher Services